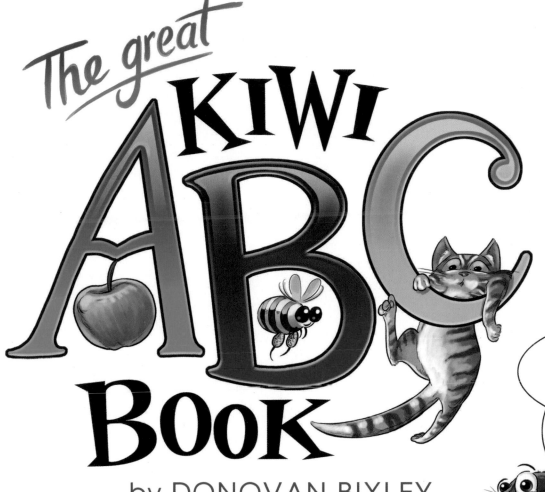

The great KIWI ABC Book

by DONOVAN BIXLEY

Find me on every page

A catalogue record for this book is available from the National Library of New Zealand

ISBN 978-1-927262-71-9

An Upstart Press Book
Published in 2016 by Upstart Press Ltd
B3, 72 Apollo Drive, Rosedale
Auckland, New Zealand

Reprinted 2017, 2018, 2021

Illustrations © Donovan Bixley 2016
Format © Upstart Press Ltd 2016

Printed by 1010 Printing International Ltd

A a

All Black lambs

apple

autumn leaves

ANZAC BISCUITS

ANZAC BISCUITS

A GRADE

AOTEAROA APPLES

B b

beach

banana

boy

bike

BUS

BABY

bulldozer

BAND

C c

cat

cow

cricket game

car

cloud

corn

CAMPGROUND

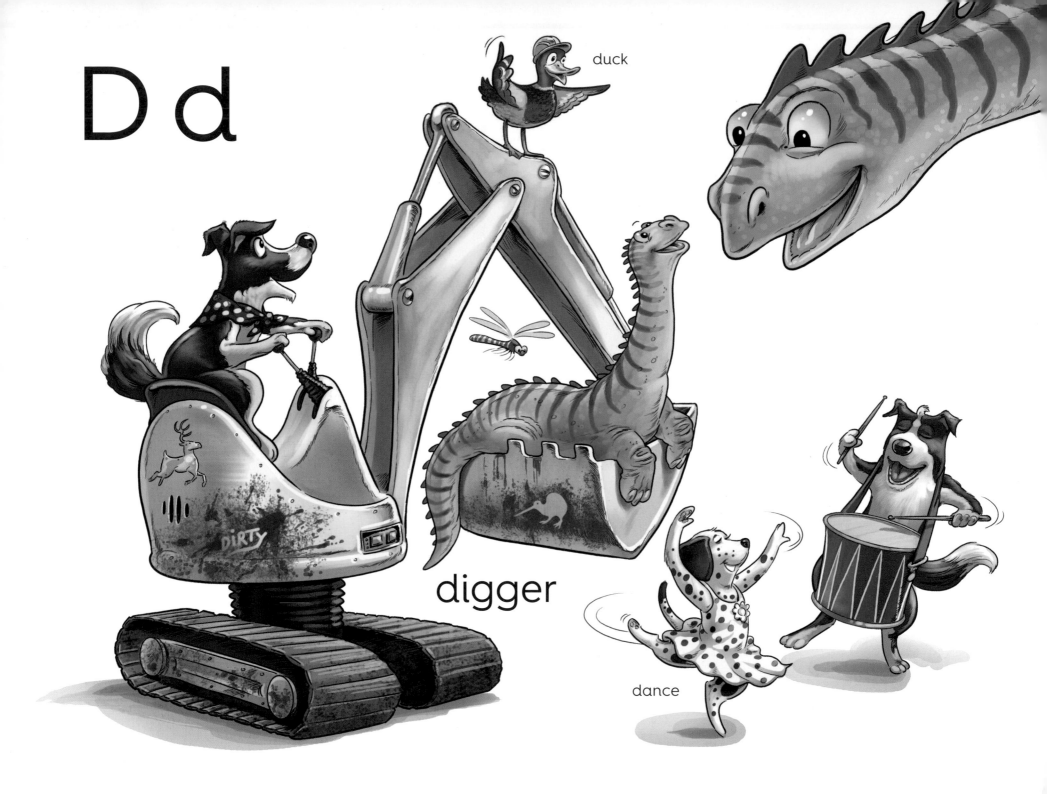

D d

duck

digger

dance

E e

ear

eggs

Easter Egg

sender:
Elle Fant
E Street
Eketahuna

F f

fantail

farm

forest

flowers

fish and chips

FURRY FEET?

FREE!

G g

goat

grass

Hh

hat

Ii

ice cream

INVITATION
Come to my
cool party

ice

J j

jug

juice

K k

kea

kite

kōwhai tree

kia ora

kete

kākāpō

lighthouse

L l

leaf

lantern

lamb

ladybird

Matariki

M m

morepork

marae

mountains

mist

moth

magpie

MILK SHAKE

MAP of New Zealand

MAX

N n

nīkau palm

netball

nest

oystercatcher

ocean

orca

O o

outboard motor

orchard

P p

paper plane

pōhutukawa

penguin

Picasso

pavlova

poi

PLAYGROUND

poppy

Q q

QUEUE

Queen

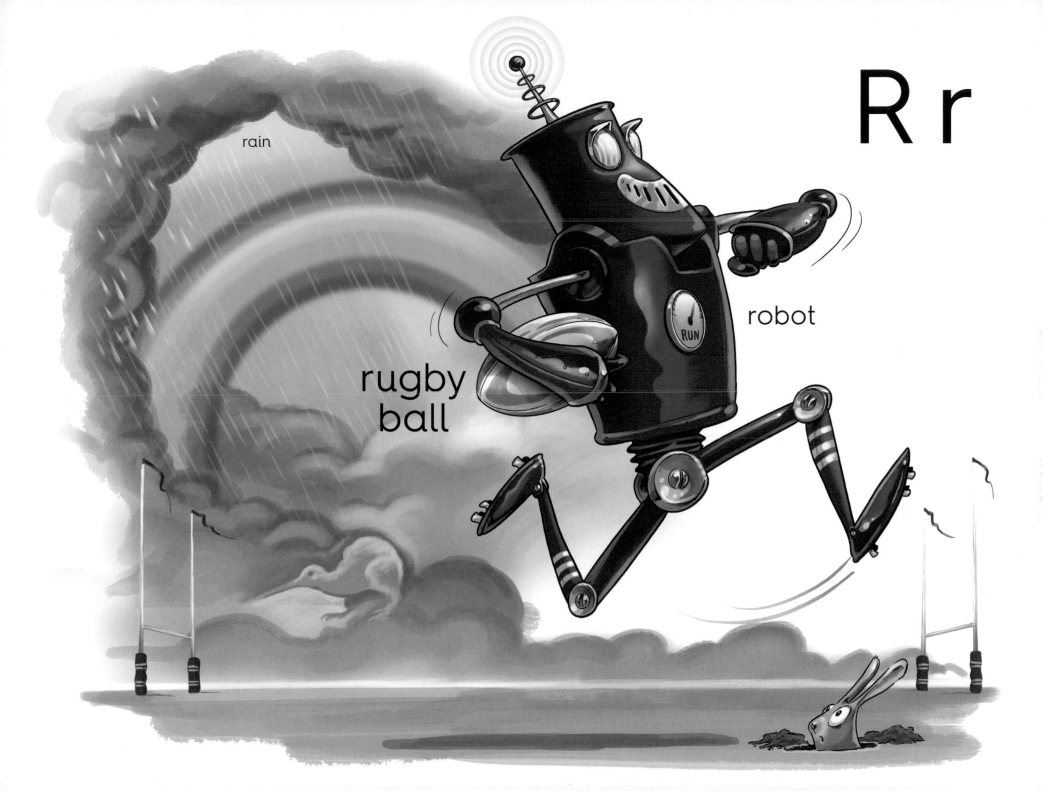

rain

robot

rugby ball

R r

S s

SKI SLOPE
SPEEDY SIGNS

snowman

ski bunny

sheep

squid

snowflakes

Tt

turkey

tractor

tuatara

tyre

tūī

U u

unicorn

unicycle

V v

volcano

valley

W w

waterfall

waka

wētā

weka

X x

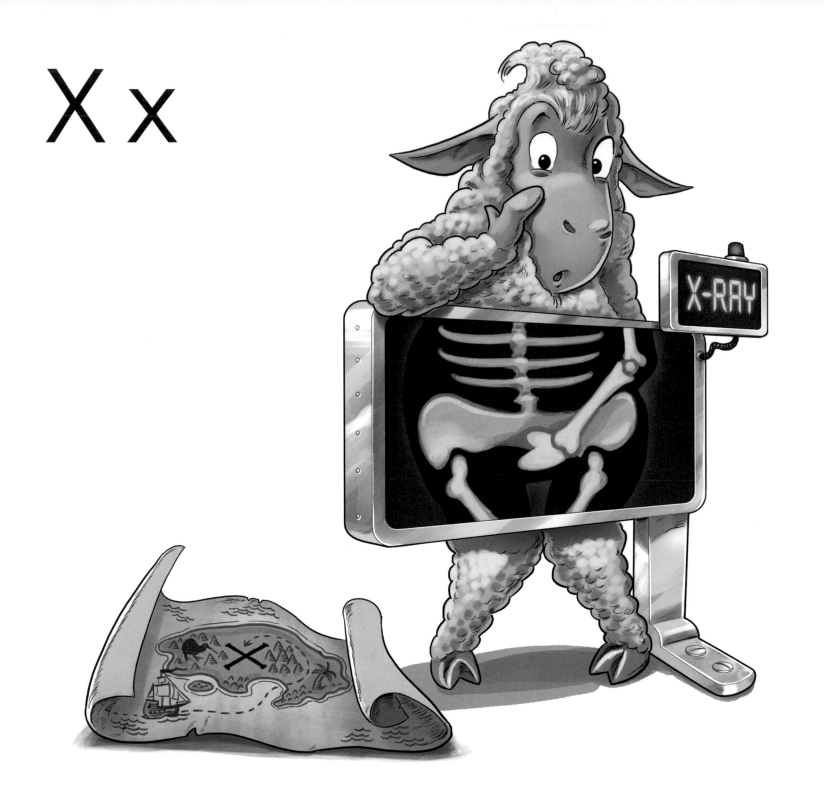